I love to stand up paddle board because:

Key: ☐ Sea ☐ Canal ☐ Lake ☐ River

MONTH_____ ☐ ☐ ☐
☐	☐	☐	☐	☐	☐
☐	☐	☐	☐	☐	☐
☐	☐	☐	☐	☐	☐
☐	☐	☐	☐	☐	☐

MONTH_____ ☐ ☐ ☐
☐	☐	☐	☐	☐	☐
☐	☐	☐	☐	☐	☐
☐	☐	☐	☐	☐	☐
☐	☐	☐	☐	☐	☐

MONTH_____ ☐ ☐ ☐
☐	☐	☐	☐	☐	☐
☐	☐	☐	☐	☐	☐
☐	☐	☐	☐	☐	☐
☐	☐	☐	☐	☐	☐

MONTH_____ ☐ ☐ ☐
☐	☐	☐	☐	☐	☐
☐	☐	☐	☐	☐	☐
☐	☐	☐	☐	☐	☐
☐	☐	☐	☐	☐	☐

MONTH_____ ☐ ☐ ☐
☐	☐	☐	☐	☐	☐
☐	☐	☐	☐	☐	☐
☐	☐	☐	☐	☐	☐
☐	☐	☐	☐	☐	☐

MONTH_____ ☐ ☐ ☐
☐	☐	☐	☐	☐	☐
☐	☐	☐	☐	☐	☐
☐	☐	☐	☐	☐	☐
☐	☐	☐	☐	☐	☐

Notes:

Key: ☐ Sea ☐ Canal ☐ Lake ☐ River

MONTH_____ ☐ ☐ ☐

☐ ☐ ☐ ☐ ☐ ☐ ☐
☐ ☐ ☐ ☐ ☐ ☐ ☐
☐ ☐ ☐ ☐ ☐ ☐ ☐
☐ ☐ ☐ ☐ ☐ ☐ ☐

MONTH_____ ☐ ☐ ☐

☐ ☐ ☐ ☐ ☐ ☐ ☐
☐ ☐ ☐ ☐ ☐ ☐ ☐
☐ ☐ ☐ ☐ ☐ ☐ ☐
☐ ☐ ☐ ☐ ☐ ☐ ☐

MONTH_____ ☐ ☐ ☐

☐ ☐ ☐ ☐ ☐ ☐ ☐
☐ ☐ ☐ ☐ ☐ ☐ ☐
☐ ☐ ☐ ☐ ☐ ☐ ☐
☐ ☐ ☐ ☐ ☐ ☐ ☐

MONTH_____ ☐ ☐ ☐

☐ ☐ ☐ ☐ ☐ ☐ ☐
☐ ☐ ☐ ☐ ☐ ☐ ☐
☐ ☐ ☐ ☐ ☐ ☐ ☐
☐ ☐ ☐ ☐ ☐ ☐ ☐

MONTH_____ ☐ ☐ ☐

☐ ☐ ☐ ☐ ☐ ☐ ☐
☐ ☐ ☐ ☐ ☐ ☐ ☐
☐ ☐ ☐ ☐ ☐ ☐ ☐
☐ ☐ ☐ ☐ ☐ ☐ ☐

MONTH_____ ☐ ☐ ☐

☐ ☐ ☐ ☐ ☐ ☐ ☐
☐ ☐ ☐ ☐ ☐ ☐ ☐
☐ ☐ ☐ ☐ ☐ ☐ ☐
☐ ☐ ☐ ☐ ☐ ☐ ☐

Notes:

Date: .... Time: ....

Air Temp: ....

Location: ....

Launch Point: ....

Type:
Canal ☐ Sea ☐
River ☐ Lake ☐

Weather:
☀ ☐ ☁ ☐
⛅ ☐ 🌧 ☐
☁ ☐ 🌧 ☐

Details:

Statistics:

Distance:

Time:

Difficulty:

Beginner ———— Challenging

○ ○ ○ ○ ○

Conditions:

....

....

....

....

....

Date: .... Time: ....

Air Temp: ....

Location: ....

Launch Point: ....

Type:
| Canal ☐ | Sea ☐ |
| River ☐ | Lake ☐ |

Weather:
☀ ☐	☁ ☐
⛅ ☐	🌧 ☐
☁ ☐	🌧 ☐

Details:

Statistics:

Distance:

Time:

Difficulty:

Beginner ——————— Challenging

○ ○ ○ ○ ○

Conditions:

....

....

....

....

....

Date: .... Time: ....

Type:

Canal	☐	Sea	☐
River	☐	Lake	☐

Air Temp: ....

Location: ....

Launch Point: ....

Weather:

☀	☐	☁	☐
⛅	☐	🌦	☐
☁	☐	🌧	☐

Details:

Statistics:

Distance:

Time:

Difficulty:

Beginner ——————— Challenging

◯ ◯ ◯ ◯ ◯

Conditions:

....

....

....

....

....

Date: .... Time: ....

Air Temp: ....

Location: ....

Launch Point: ....

Type:
Canal ☐ Sea ☐
River ☐ Lake ☐

Weather:
☀ ☐   ☁ ☐
⛅ ☐   🌧 ☐
☁ ☐   🌧 ☐

Details:

Statistics:

Distance:

Time:

Difficulty:

Beginner ———— Challenging

○ ○ ○ ○ ○

Conditions:

....

....

....

....

....

Date: .... Time: ....

Air Temp: ....

Location: ....

Launch Point: ....

Type:

Canal ☐	Sea ☐
River ☐	Lake ☐

Weather:

☀ ☐   ☁ ☐

⛅ ☐   🌧 ☐

☁ ☐   🌧 ☐

Details:

Statistics:

Distance:

Time:

Difficulty:

Beginner ———— Challenging

○ ○ ○ ○ ○

Conditions:

....

....

....

....

....

Date: .... Time: ....

Air Temp: ....

Location: ....

Launch Point: ....

Type:

Canal ☐   Sea ☐
River ☐   Lake ☐

Weather:

☀ ☐   ☁ ☐
⛅ ☐   🌧 ☐
☁ ☐   🌧 ☐

Details:

Statistics:

Distance:

Time:

Difficulty:

Beginner ——————— Challenging

◯ ◯ ◯ ◯ ◯

Conditions:

....

....

....

....

....

Date: _____ Time: _____

Air Temp: _____

Location: _____

Launch Point: _____

Type:

Canal ☐	Sea ☐
River ☐	Lake ☐

Weather:

☀ ☐   ☁ ☐
⛅ ☐   🌧 ☐
☁ ☐   🌦 ☐

Details:

Statistics:

Distance:

Time:

Difficulty:

Beginner ———— Challenging

○ ○ ○ ○ ○

Conditions:

_____

_____

_____

_____

_____

Date: .... Time: ....

Air Temp: ....

Location: ....

Launch Point: ....

Type: Canal ☐ Sea ☐
River ☐ Lake ☐

Weather: ☀ ☐ ☁ ☐
⛅ ☐ 🌧 ☐
☁ ☐ 🌧 ☐

Details:

Statistics:

Distance:

Time:

Difficulty:

Beginner ———— Challenging
○ ○ ○ ○ ○

Conditions:

....

....

....

....

....

Date: .... Time: ....

Air Temp: ....

Location: ....

Launch Point: ....

Type:
| Canal ☐ | Sea ☐ |
| River ☐ | Lake ☐ |

Weather:

☀ ☐   ☁ ☐

⛅ ☐   🌧 ☐

☁ ☐   🌧 ☐

Details:

Statistics:

Distance:

Time:

Difficulty:

Beginner ———— Challenging

○ ○ ○ ○ ○

Conditions:

....

....

....

....

....

Date: .... Time: ....

Canal ☐	Sea ☐
River ☐	Lake ☐

Air Temp: ....

Location: ....

Launch Point: ....

Weather:

☀ ☐   ☁ ☐

⛅ ☐   🌧 ☐

☁ ☐   🌧 ☐

Details:

Statistics:

Distance:

Time:

Difficulty:

Beginner ———————— Challenging

◯ ◯ ◯ ◯ ◯

Conditions:

....

....

....

....

....

Date: _____ Time: _____

Air Temp: _____

Location: _____

Launch Point: _____

Type:

| Canal ☐ | Sea ☐ |
| River ☐ | Lake ☐ |

Weather:

☀ ☐ ☁ ☐
⛅ ☐ 🌧 ☐
☁ ☐ 🌧 ☐

Details:

Statistics:

Distance:

Time:

Difficulty:

Beginner ———— Challenging

○ ○ ○ ○ ○

Conditions:

_____

_____

_____

_____

_____

Date: .... Time: ....

Air Temp: ....

Location: ....

Launch Point: ....

Type:
| Canal ☐ | Sea ☐ |
| River ☐ | Lake ☐ |

Weather:
☀ ☐	☁ ☐
🌤 ☐	🌧 ☐
☁ ☐	🌧 ☐

Details:

Statistics:

Distance:

Time:

Difficulty:

Beginner ——— Challenging

◯ ◯ ◯ ◯ ◯

Conditions:

....

....

....

....

....

Date: .... Time: ....

Air Temp: ....

Location: ....

Launch Point: ....

Type:
Canal ☐ Sea ☐
River ☐ Lake ☐

Weather:
☀ ☐   ☁ ☐
⛅ ☐   🌧 ☐
☁ ☐   🌧 ☐

Details:

Statistics:

Distance:

Time:

Difficulty:

Beginner ———— Challenging

○ ○ ○ ○ ○

Conditions:

....

....

....

....

....

Date: .... Time: ....

Air Temp: ....

Location: ....

Launch Point: ....

Type:

Canal ☐	Sea ☐
River ☐	Lake ☐

Weather:

☀ ☐	☁ ☐
⛅ ☐	🌧 ☐
☁ ☐	🌧 ☐

Details:

Statistics:

Distance:

Time:

Difficulty:

Beginner ——————— Challenging

○ ○ ○ ○ ○

Conditions:

....

....

....

....

....

Date: .... Time: ....

Air Temp: ....

Location: ....

Launch Point: ....

Type:
Canal ☐ Sea ☐
River ☐ Lake ☐

Weather:
☀ ☐   ☁ ☐
⛅ ☐   🌧 ☐
☁ ☐   🌧 ☐

Details:

Statistics:
Distance:
Time:

Difficulty:
Beginner ——————— Challenging
○ ○ ○ ○ ○

Conditions:
....
....
....
....
....

Date: .... Time: ....

Air Temp: ....

Location: ....

Launch Point: ....

Type:

| Canal ☐ | Sea ☐ |
| River ☐ | Lake ☐ |

Weather:

☀ ☐	☁ ☐
⛅ ☐	🌧 ☐
☁ ☐	🌧 ☐

Details:

Statistics:

Distance:

Time:

Conditions:

....

....

....

....

....

Difficulty:

Beginner ———— Challenging

○ ○ ○ ○ ○

Date: _____ Time: _____

Air Temp: _____

Location: _____

Launch Point: _____

Type:
Canal ☐ Sea ☐
River ☐ Lake ☐

Weather:
☀ ☐   ☁ ☐
⛅ ☐   🌧 ☐
☁ ☐   🌧 ☐

Details:

Statistics:
Distance:
Time:

Difficulty:
Beginner ——————— Challenging
◯ ◯ ◯ ◯ ◯

Conditions:
_____
_____
_____
_____
_____

Date: .... Time: ....

Air Temp: ....

Location: ....

Launch Point: ....

Canal ☐ Sea ☐
River ☐ Lake ☐

Weather:

☀ ☐   ☁ ☐
⛅ ☐   🌧 ☐
☁ ☐   🌧 ☐

Details:

Statistics:

Distance:

Time:

Conditions:

....

....

....

....

....

Difficulty:

Beginner ————— Challenging

○ ○ ○ ○ ○

Date: .... Time: ....

Canal ☐ Sea ☐
River ☐ Lake ☐

Air Temp: ....

Weather:
☀ ☐   ☁ ☐
⛅ ☐   🌧 ☐
☁ ☐   🌧 ☐

Location: ....

Launch Point: ....

Details:

Statistics:

Distance:

Time:

Difficulty:

Beginner ———— Challenging

○ ○ ○ ○ ○

Conditions:

....

....

....

....

....

Date: .... Time: ....

Air Temp: ....

Location: ....

Launch Point: ....

Type: Canal ☐ Sea ☐ River ☐ Lake ☐

Weather: ☀ ☐ ☁ ☐ ⛅ ☐ 🌧 ☐ ☁ ☐ 🌧 ☐

Details:

Statistics:

Distance:

Time:

Difficulty:

Beginner ——— Challenging

○ ○ ○ ○ ○

Conditions:

....

....

....

....

....

Date: _____ Time: _____

Air Temp: _____

Location: _____

Launch Point: _____

Type:
- Canal ☐ Sea ☐
- River ☐ Lake ☐

Weather:
- ☀ ☐   ☁ ☐
- ⛅ ☐   🌧 ☐
- ☁ ☐   🌧 ☐

Details:

Statistics:
Distance:
Time:

Difficulty:
Beginner ———— Challenging
○ ○ ○ ○ ○

Conditions:
_____
_____
_____
_____
_____

Date: .... Time: ....

Air Temp: ....

Location: ....

Launch Point: ....

Type:
Canal ☐ Sea ☐
River ☐ Lake ☐

Weather:
☀ ☐   ☁ ☐
⛅ ☐   🌧 ☐
☁ ☐   🌧 ☐

Details:

Statistics:
Distance:
Time:

Difficulty:
Beginner ———— Challenging
○ ○ ○ ○ ○

Conditions:

....

....

....

....

....

Date: .... Time: ....

Air Temp: ....

Location: ....

Launch Point: ....

Type:
Canal ☐ Sea ☐
River ☐ Lake ☐

Weather:
☀ ☐   ☁ ☐
⛅ ☐   🌧 ☐
☁ ☐   🌧 ☐

Details:

Statistics:

Distance:

Time:

Difficulty:

Beginner ———— Challenging

◯ ◯ ◯ ◯ ◯

Conditions:

....

....

....

....

....

Date: _____ Time: _____

Air Temp: _____

Location: _____

Launch Point: _____

Type:
Canal ☐   Sea ☐
River ☐   Lake ☐

Weather:
☀ ☐   ☁ ☐
⛅ ☐   🌧 ☐
☁ ☐   🌧 ☐

Details:

Statistics:

Distance:

Time:

Difficulty:

Beginner ——————— Challenging
◯ ◯ ◯ ◯ ◯

Conditions:

_____

_____

_____

_____

_____

Date: .... Time: ....

Air Temp: ....

Location: ....

Launch Point: ....

Canal ☐   Sea ☐
River ☐   Lake ☐

Weather:
☀ ☐   ☁ ☐
⛅ ☐   🌧 ☐
☁ ☐   🌧 ☐

Details:

Statistics:

Distance:

Time:

Difficulty:

Beginner ——————— Challenging

◯ ◯ ◯ ◯ ◯

Conditions:

....

....

....

....

....

Date: _____ Time: _____

Air Temp: _____

Location: _____

Launch Point: _____

Type:
Canal ☐ Sea ☐
River ☐ Lake ☐

Weather:
☀ ☐   ☁ ☐
⛅ ☐   🌧 ☐
☁ ☐   🌧 ☐

Details:

Statistics:

Distance:

Time:

Difficulty:

Beginner ——————— Challenging

○ ○ ○ ○ ○

Conditions:

_____

_____

_____

_____

_____

Date: .... Time: ....

Air Temp: ....

Location: ....

Launch Point: ....

Canal ☐ Sea ☐
River ☐ Lake ☐

Weather:
☀ ☐   ☁ ☐
⛅ ☐   🌧 ☐
☁ ☐   🌧 ☐

Details:

Statistics:
Distance:
Time:

Difficulty:
Beginner ———— Challenging
◯ ◯ ◯ ◯ ◯

Conditions:
....
....
....
....
....

Date: _____ Time: _____

Air Temp: _____

Location: _____

Launch Point: _____

Type:
Canal ☐ Sea ☐
River ☐ Lake ☐

Weather:
☀ ☐ ☁ ☐
⛅ ☐ 🌦 ☐
☁ ☐ 🌧 ☐

Details:

Statistics:
Distance:
Time:

Difficulty:
Beginner ———— Challenging
◯ ◯ ◯ ◯ ◯

Conditions:
_____
_____
_____
_____
_____

Date: _____ Time: _____

Type:

Canal ☐ Sea ☐
River ☐ Lake ☐

Air Temp: _____

Location: _____

Launch Point: _____

Weather:

☀ ☐   ☁ ☐

⛅ ☐   🌧 ☐

☁ ☐   🌧 ☐

Details:

Statistics:

Distance:

Time:

Difficulty:

Beginner ———— Challenging

◯ ◯ ◯ ◯ ◯

Conditions:

_____

_____

_____

_____

_____

Date: .... Time: ....

Air Temp: ....

Location: ....

Launch Point: ....

Type:
Canal ☐ Sea ☐
River ☐ Lake ☐

Weather:
☀ ☐ ☁ ☐
⛅ ☐ 🌧 ☐
☁ ☐ ⛈ ☐

Details:

Statistics:

Distance:

Time:

Conditions:

....

....

....

Difficulty:

Beginner ———— Challenging

◯ ◯ ◯ ◯ ◯

....

....

Date: .... Time: ....

Canal ☐ Sea ☐
River ☐ Lake ☐

Air Temp: ....

Weather:
☀ ☐   ☁ ☐
⛅ ☐   🌧 ☐
☁ ☐   🌧 ☐

Location: ....

Launch Point: ....

Details:

Statistics:

Distance:

Time:

Conditions:
....
....
....
....
....

Difficulty:

Beginner ———— Challenging

◯ ◯ ◯ ◯ ◯

Date: _____ Time: _____

Air Temp: _____

Location: _____

Launch Point: _____

| Canal ☐ | Sea ☐ |
| River ☐ | Lake ☐ |

Weather:

☀ ☐	☁ ☐
⛅ ☐	🌧 ☐
☁ ☐	🌧 ☐

Details:

Statistics:

Distance:

Time:

Difficulty:

Beginner ——————— Challenging

○ ○ ○ ○ ○

Conditions:

_____

_____

_____

_____

_____

Date: _____ Time: _____

Air Temp: _____

Location: _____

Launch Point: _____

Type:
Canal ☐	Sea ☐
River ☐	Lake ☐

Weather:
☀ ☐   ☁ ☐
⛅ ☐   🌧 ☐
☁ ☐   🌧 ☐

Details:

Statistics:

Distance:

Time:

Difficulty:

Beginner ——————— Challenging

○ ○ ○ ○ ○

Conditions:

_____

_____

_____

_____

_____

Date: .... Time: ....

Air Temp: ....

Location: ....

Launch Point: ....

Type:
Canal ☐   Sea ☐
River ☐   Lake ☐

Weather:
☀ ☐   ☁ ☐
⛅ ☐   🌧 ☐
☁ ☐   🌧 ☐

Details:

Statistics:
Distance:
Time:

Difficulty:
Beginner ———— Challenging
○ ○ ○ ○ ○

Conditions:
....
....
....
....
....

Date: _____ Time: _____

Air Temp: _____

Location: _____

Launch Point: _____

| Canal ☐ | Sea ☐ |
| River ☐ | Lake ☐ |

Weather:

☀ ☐	☁ ☐
⛅ ☐	🌧 ☐
☁ ☐	🌧 ☐

Details:

Statistics:

Distance:

Time:

Conditions:

_____

_____

_____

_____

_____

Difficulty:

Beginner ——————— Challenging

○ ○ ○ ○ ○

Date: .... Time: ....

Air Temp: ....

Location: ....

Launch Point: ....

Type:
| Canal ☐ | Sea ☐ |
| River ☐ | Lake ☐ |

Weather:
☀ ☐	☁ ☐
⛅ ☐	🌧 ☐
☁ ☐	🌧 ☐

Details:

Statistics:

Distance:

Time:

Difficulty:

Beginner ———— Challenging

○ ○ ○ ○ ○

Conditions:

....

....

....

....

....

Date: .... Time: ....

Air Temp: ....

Location: ....

Launch Point: ....

Type:
| Canal ☐ | Sea ☐ |
| River ☐ | Lake ☐ |

Weather:
☀ ☐ ☐ ☐
⛅ ☐ 🌧 ☐
☁ ☐ 🌧 ☐

Details:

Statistics:

Distance:

Time:

Difficulty:

Beginner ———— Challenging

◯ ◯ ◯ ◯ ◯

Conditions:

....

....

....

....

....

Date: .... Time: ....

Air Temp: ....

Location: ....

Launch Point: ....

Type:

Canal ☐ Sea ☐
River ☐ Lake ☐

Weather:

☀ ☐   ☁ ☐
⛅ ☐   🌧 ☐
☁ ☐   🌧 ☐

Details:

Statistics:

Distance:

Time:

Conditions:

....

....

Difficulty:

Beginner ———— Challenging

○ ○ ○ ○ ○

....

....

....

Date: .... Time: ....

Air Temp: ....

Location: ....

Launch Point: ....

Type:
Canal ☐ Sea ☐
River ☐ Lake ☐

Weather:
☀ ☐   ☁ ☐
⛅ ☐   🌧 ☐
☁ ☐   🌧 ☐

Details:

Statistics:

Distance:

Time:

Conditions:
....
....
....
....
....

Difficulty:

Beginner ——————— Challenging

◯ ◯ ◯ ◯ ◯

Date: .... Time: ....

Air Temp: ....

Location: ....

Launch Point: ....

Type:
Canal ☐   Sea ☐
River ☐   Lake ☐

Weather:
☀ ☐   ☁ ☐
⛅ ☐   🌧 ☐
☁ ☐   🌧 ☐

Details:

Statistics:

Distance:

Time:

Difficulty:

Beginner ——————— Challenging

◯ ◯ ◯ ◯ ◯

Conditions:

....

....

....

....

....

Date: .... Time: ....

Air Temp: ....

Location: ....

Launch Point: ....

Type:
Canal ☐ Sea ☐
River ☐ Lake ☐

Weather:
☀ ☐   ☁ ☐
⛅ ☐   🌧 ☐
☁ ☐   🌧 ☐

Details:

Statistics:

Distance:

Time:

Difficulty:

Beginner ———— Challenging
○ ○ ○ ○ ○

Conditions:

....

....

....

....

....

Date: .... Time: ....

Air Temp: ....

Location: ....

Launch Point: ....

Type:

| Canal ☐ | Sea ☐ |
| River ☐ | Lake ☐ |

Weather:

☀ ☐	☁ ☐
⛅ ☐	🌧 ☐
☁ ☐	⛈ ☐

Details:

Statistics:

Distance:

Time:

Difficulty:

Beginner ———— Challenging

○ ○ ○ ○ ○

Conditions:

....

....

....

....

....

Date: _____ Time: _____

| Canal ☐ | Sea ☐ |
| River ☐ | Lake ☐ |

Air Temp: _____

Location: _____

Launch Point: _____

Weather:

☀ ☐	☁ ☐
⛅ ☐	🌧 ☐
☁ ☐	🌧 ☐

Details:

Statistics:

Distance:

Time:

Difficulty:

Beginner ——————— Challenging

◯ ◯ ◯ ◯ ◯

Conditions:

_____

_____

_____

_____

_____

Date: .... Time: ....

Air Temp: ....

Location: ....

Launch Point: ....

Type:
Canal ☐ Sea ☐
River ☐ Lake ☐

Weather:
☀ ☐   ☁ ☐
⛅ ☐   🌧 ☐
☁ ☐   🌧 ☐

Details:

Statistics:

Distance:

Time:

Difficulty:

Beginner ———— Challenging

○ ○ ○ ○ ○

Conditions:

....

....

....

....

....

Date: .... Time: ....

Air Temp: ....

Location: ....

Launch Point: ....

Canal ☐ Sea ☐
River ☐ Lake ☐

Weather:

☀ ☐ ☁ ☐
⛅ ☐ 🌧 ☐
☁ ☐ 🌧 ☐

Details:

Statistics:

Distance:

Time:

Conditions:

....

....

Difficulty:

Beginner ———— Challenging

◯ ◯ ◯ ◯ ◯

....

....

....

Date: .... Time: ....

Air Temp: ....

Location: ....

Launch Point: ....

Canal ☐ Sea ☐
River ☐ Lake ☐

Weather:

☀ ☐   ☁ ☐
⛅ ☐   🌧 ☐
☁ ☐   🌧 ☐

Details:

Statistics:

Distance:

Time:

Difficulty:

Beginner ——————— Challenging

◯ ◯ ◯ ◯ ◯

Conditions:

....

....

....

....

....

Date: .... Time: ....

Air Temp: ....

Location: ....

Launch Point: ....

Type:

Canal ☐   Sea ☐
River ☐   Lake ☐

Weather:

☀ ☐   ☁ ☐
⛅ ☐   🌧 ☐
☁ ☐   🌧 ☐

Details:

Statistics:

Distance:

Time:

Conditions:

....

....

Difficulty:

Beginner ———— Challenging

◯ ◯ ◯ ◯ ◯

....

....

....

Date: .... Time: ....

Air Temp: ....

Location: ....

Launch Point: ....

Type:

Canal ☐	Sea ☐
River ☐	Lake ☐

Weather:

☀ ☐   ☁ ☐
⛅ ☐   🌧 ☐
☁ ☐   🌧 ☐

Details:

Statistics:

Distance:

Time:

Difficulty:

Beginner ———— Challenging

◯ ◯ ◯ ◯ ◯

Conditions:

....

....

....

....

....

Date: .... Time: ....

Air Temp: ....

Location: ....

Launch Point: ....

Type:
Canal ☐ Sea ☐
River ☐ Lake ☐

Weather:
☀ ☐   ☁ ☐
⛅ ☐   🌧 ☐
☁ ☐   🌧 ☐

Details:

Statistics:

Distance:

Time:

Difficulty:

Beginner ———— Challenging

◯ ◯ ◯ ◯ ◯

Conditions:

....

....

....

....

....

Date: .... Time: ....

Air Temp: ....

Location: ....

Launch Point: ....

Type:
| Canal ☐ | Sea ☐ |
| River ☐ | Lake ☐ |

Weather:
☀ ☐   ☁ ☐
⛅ ☐   🌧 ☐
☁ ☐   🌧 ☐

Details:

Statistics:

Distance:

Time:

Difficulty:

Beginner ———— Challenging

○ ○ ○ ○ ○

Conditions:

....

....

....

....

....

Date: .... Time: ....

Air Temp: ....

Location: ....

Launch Point: ....

Type:
Canal ☐ Sea ☐
River ☐ Lake ☐

Weather:
☀ ☐   ☁ ☐
⛅ ☐   🌧 ☐
☁ ☐   🌧 ☐

Details:

Statistics:

Distance:

Time:

Conditions:
....
....
....
....
....

Difficulty:

Beginner ————— Challenging

◯ ◯ ◯ ◯ ◯

Date: .... Time: ....

Air Temp: ....

Location: ....

Launch Point: ....

Type:
Canal ☐ Sea ☐
River ☐ Lake ☐

Weather:
☀ ☐   ☁ ☐
⛅ ☐   🌧 ☐
☁ ☐   🌧 ☐

Details:

Statistics:
Distance:
Time:

Difficulty:
Beginner ———— Challenging
◯ ◯ ◯ ◯ ◯

Conditions:
....
....
....
....
....

Date: .... Time: ....

Air Temp: ....

Location: ....

Launch Point: ....

Type:
Canal ☐ Sea ☐
River ☐ Lake ☐

Weather:
☀ ☐   ☁ ☐
⛅ ☐   🌦 ☐
☁ ☐   🌧 ☐

Details:

Statistics:

Distance:

Time:

Difficulty:

Beginner ————— Challenging

○ ○ ○ ○ ○

Conditions:

....

....

....

....

....

Date: .... Time: ....

Air Temp: ....

Location: ....

Launch Point: ....

Type: Canal ☐ Sea ☐ River ☐ Lake ☐

Weather: ☐ ☐ ☐ ☐ ☐ ☐ ☐ ☐ ☐ ☐ ☐ ☐

Details:

Statistics:

Distance:

Time:

Conditions:

....

....

....

....

....

Difficulty:

Beginner ——————— Challenging

◯ ◯ ◯ ◯ ◯

Date: .... Time: ....

Air Temp: ....

Location: ....

Launch Point: ....

Type:

Canal ☐ Sea ☐
River ☐ Lake ☐

Weather:

☀ ☐   ☁ ☐
⛅ ☐   🌧 ☐
☁ ☐   🌧 ☐

Details:

Statistics:

Distance:

Time:

Difficulty:

Beginner ——————— Challenging

◯ ◯ ◯ ◯ ◯

Conditions:

....

....

....

....

....

Date: .... Time: ....

Air Temp: ....

Location: ....

Launch Point: ....

Type:
| Canal ☐ | Sea ☐ |
| River ☐ | Lake ☐ |

Weather:
☀ ☐	☁ ☐
⛅ ☐	🌧 ☐
☁ ☐	🌧 ☐

Details:

Statistics:

Distance:

Time:

Conditions:

....

....

....

....

....

Difficulty:

Beginner ——————— Challenging

◯ ◯ ◯ ◯ ◯

Date: .... Time: ....

Air Temp: ....

Location: ....

Launch Point: ....

Canal ☐		Sea ☐	
River ☐		Lake ☐	

Weather:

☀ ☐	☁ ☐
⛅ ☐	🌧 ☐
☁ ☐	🌧 ☐

Details:

Statistics:

Distance:

Time:

Difficulty:

Beginner ———————— Challenging

○ ○ ○ ○ ○

Conditions:

....

....

....

....

....

Date: _____ Time: _____

Air Temp: _____

Location: _____

Launch Point: _____

Type:

Canal	☐	Sea	☐
River	☐	Lake	☐

Weather:

☀	☐	☁	☐
⛅	☐	🌧	☐
☁	☐	🌧	☐

Details:

Statistics:

Distance:

Time:

Difficulty:

Beginner ——————— Challenging

○ ○ ○ ○ ○

Conditions:

_____

_____

_____

_____

_____

Date: .... Time: ....

Air Temp: ....

Location: ....

Launch Point: ....

Type:

Canal ☐	Sea ☐
River ☐	Lake ☐

Weather:

☀ ☐   ☁ ☐

⛅ ☐   🌧 ☐

☁ ☐   🌧 ☐

Details:

Statistics:

Distance:

Time:

Conditions:

....

....

....

....

....

Difficulty:

Beginner ———— Challenging

○ ○ ○ ○ ○

Date: .... Time: ....

Air Temp: ....

Location: ....

Launch Point: ....

Type:

Canal ☐ Sea ☐
River ☐ Lake ☐

Weather:

☀ ☐   ☁ ☐
⛅ ☐   🌧 ☐
☁ ☐   🌧 ☐

Details:

Statistics:

Distance:

Time:

Difficulty:

Beginner ————— Challenging

◯ ◯ ◯ ◯ ◯

Conditions:

....

....

....

....

....

Date: _____ Time: _____

Air Temp: _____

Location: _____

Launch Point: _____

Canal ☐ Sea ☐
River ☐ Lake ☐

Weather:

☀ ☐   ☁ ☐
⛅ ☐   🌧 ☐
☁ ☐   🌧 ☐

Details:

Statistics:

Distance:

Time:

Difficulty:

Beginner ———— Challenging

○ ○ ○ ○ ○

Conditions:

_____

_____

_____

_____

_____

Date: .... Time: ....

Air Temp: ....

Location: ....

Launch Point: ....

Type:

Canal ☐ Sea ☐
River ☐ Lake ☐

Weather:

☀ ☐   ☁ ☐
⛅ ☐   🌧 ☐
☁ ☐   🌧 ☐

Details:

Statistics:

Distance:

Time:

Difficulty:

Beginner ——— Challenging

○ ○ ○ ○ ○

Conditions:

....

....

....

....

....

Date: .... Time: ....

Air Temp: ....

Location: ....

Launch Point: ....

Type: Canal ☐ Sea ☐ River ☐ Lake ☐

Weather: ☀ ☐ ☁ ☐ ⛅ ☐ 🌦 ☐ ☁ ☐ 🌧 ☐

Details:

Statistics:

Distance:

Time:

Difficulty:

Beginner ———— Challenging

○ ○ ○ ○ ○

Conditions:

....

....

....

....

....

Date: .... Time: ....

Air Temp: ....

Location: ....

Launch Point: ....

Type:

| Canal ☐ | Sea ☐ |
| River ☐ | Lake ☐ |

Weather:

☀ ☐   ☁ ☐
⛅ ☐   🌧 ☐
☁ ☐   🌧 ☐

Details:

Statistics:

Distance:

Time:

Difficulty:

Beginner ——————— Challenging

◯ ◯ ◯ ◯ ◯

Conditions:

....

....

....

....

....

Date: .... Time: ....

Air Temp: ....

Location: ....

Launch Point: ....

Type:
Canal ☐   Sea ☐
River ☐   Lake ☐

Weather:
☀ ☐   ☁ ☐
⛅ ☐   🌧 ☐
☁ ☐   🌧 ☐

Details:

Statistics:

Distance:

Time:

Conditions:

....

....

....

....

....

Difficulty:

Beginner ———— Challenging

◯ ◯ ◯ ◯ ◯

Date: .... Time: ....

Air Temp: ....

Location: ....

Launch Point: ....

Type:

Canal ☐   Sea ☐
River ☐   Lake ☐

Weather:

☀ ☐   ☁ ☐
⛅ ☐   🌦 ☐
☁ ☐   🌧 ☐

Details:

Statistics:

Distance:

Time:

Difficulty:

Beginner ——————— Challenging

◯ ◯ ◯ ◯ ◯

Conditions:

....

....

....

....

....

Date: .... Time: ....

Air Temp: ....

Location: ....

Launch Point: ....

Details:

Statistics:

Distance:

Time:

Difficulty:

Beginner ———— Challenging

◯ ◯ ◯ ◯ ◯

Conditions:

Date: .... Time: ....

Air Temp: ....

Location: ....

Launch Point: ....

Canal ☐ Sea ☐
River ☐ Lake ☐

Weather:

☀ ☐ ☁ ☐
⛅ ☐ 🌧 ☐
☁ ☐ 🌧 ☐

Details:

Statistics:

Distance:

Time:

Difficulty:

Beginner ———— Challenging

○ ○ ○ ○ ○

Conditions:

....

....

....

....

....

Date: .... Time: ....

Air Temp: ....

Location: ....

Launch Point: ....

Type:
Canal ☐ Sea ☐
River ☐ Lake ☐

Weather:
☀ ☐   ☁ ☐
⛅ ☐   🌧 ☐
☁ ☐   🌧 ☐

Details:

Statistics:

Distance:

Time:

Conditions:

....

....

....

....

....

Difficulty:

Beginner ———————— Challenging

◯ ◯ ◯ ◯ ◯

Date: .... Time: ....

Air Temp: ....

Location: ....

Launch Point: ....

Type:
| Canal ☐ | Sea ☐ |
| River ☐ | Lake ☐ |

Weather:
☀ ☐	☁ ☐
⛅ ☐	🌧 ☐
☁ ☐	🌧 ☐

Details:

Statistics:

Distance:

Time:

Difficulty:

Beginner ——————— Challenging

○ ○ ○ ○ ○

Conditions:

....

....

....

....

....

Date: .... Time: ....

Air Temp: ....

Location: ....

Launch Point: ....

Type:
Canal ☐ Sea ☐
River ☐ Lake ☐

Weather:
☀ ☐   ☁ ☐
⛅ ☐   🌧 ☐
☁ ☐   🌧 ☐

Details:

Statistics:
Distance:
Time:

Difficulty:
Beginner ——————— Challenging
○ ○ ○ ○ ○

Conditions:
....
....
....
....
....

Date: .... Time: ....

Air Temp: ....

Location: ....

Launch Point: ....

Type:

| Canal ☐ | Sea ☐ |
| River ☐ | Lake ☐ |

Weather:

☀ ☐	☁ ☐
⛅ ☐	🌧 ☐
☁ ☐	🌧 ☐

Details:

Statistics:

Distance:

Time:

Difficulty:

Beginner ——————— Challenging

◯ ◯ ◯ ◯ ◯

Conditions:

....

....

....

....

....

Date: .... Time: ....

Air Temp: ....

Location: ....

Launch Point: ....

Type:
Canal ☐ Sea ☐
River ☐ Lake ☐

Weather:
☀ ☐   ☁ ☐
⛅ ☐   🌧 ☐
☁ ☐   🌧 ☐

Details:

Statistics:

Distance:
Time:

Difficulty:

Beginner ——————— Challenging
○ ○ ○ ○ ○

Conditions:

....

....

....

....

....

Date: .... Time: ....

Air Temp: ....

Location: ....

Launch Point: ....

Type: Canal ☐ Sea ☐ River ☐ Lake ☐

Weather: ☀ ☐ ☁ ☐ ⛅ ☐ 🌦 ☐ ☁ ☐ 🌧 ☐

Details:

Statistics:

Distance:

Time:

Difficulty:

Beginner ————— Challenging

○ ○ ○ ○ ○

Conditions:

Date: .... Time: ....

Air Temp: ....

Location: ....

Launch Point: ....

Type:

| Canal ☐ | Sea ☐ |
| River ☐ | Lake ☐ |

Weather:

☀ ☐   ☁ ☐

⛅ ☐   🌧 ☐

☁ ☐   🌧 ☐

Details:

Statistics:

Distance:

Time:

Difficulty:

Beginner ——————— Challenging

◯ ◯ ◯ ◯ ◯

Conditions:

....

....

....

....

....

Date: .... Time: ....

Air Temp: ....

Location: ....

Launch Point: ....

Type:
Canal ☐ Sea ☐
River ☐ Lake ☐

Weather:
☀ ☐   ☁ ☐
⛅ ☐   🌧 ☐
☁ ☐   🌧 ☐

Details:

Statistics:

Distance:

Time:

Difficulty:

Beginner ——————— Challenging

○ ○ ○ ○ ○

Conditions:

....

....

....

....

....

Date: .... Time: ....

Air Temp: ....

Location: ....

Launch Point: ....

Canal ☐   Sea ☐
River ☐   Lake ☐

Weather:

☀ ☐   ☁ ☐
⛅ ☐   🌧 ☐
☁ ☐   🌧 ☐

Details:

Statistics:

Distance:

Time:

Conditions:

....

....

....

....

....

Difficulty:

Beginner ——————— Challenging

○ ○ ○ ○ ○

Date: .... Time: ....

Air Temp: ....

Location: ....

Launch Point: ....

Type: Canal ☐ Sea ☐ River ☐ Lake ☐

Weather: ☀ ☐ ☁ ☐ ⛅ ☐ 🌧 ☐ ☁ ☐ 🌧 ☐

Details:

Statistics:

Distance:

Time:

Difficulty:

Beginner ————— Challenging

○ ○ ○ ○ ○

Conditions:

....

....

....

....

....

Date: .... Time: ....

Air Temp: ....

Location: ....

Launch Point: ....

Type: Canal ☐ Sea ☐ River ☐ Lake ☐

Weather: ☀ ☐ ☁ ☐ / ⛅ ☐ 🌧 ☐ / ☁ ☐ 🌧 ☐

Details:

Statistics:

Distance:

Time:

Difficulty:

Beginner ——— Challenging

◯ ◯ ◯ ◯ ◯

Conditions:

....

....

....

....

....

Date: .... Time: ....

Air Temp: ....

Location: ....

Launch Point: ....

Canal ☐ Sea ☐
River ☐ Lake ☐

Weather:

☼ ☐   ☁ ☐
⛅ ☐   🌧 ☐
☁ ☐   🌧 ☐

Details:

Statistics:

Distance:

Time:

Difficulty:

Beginner ——————— Challenging

○ ○ ○ ○ ○

Conditions:

....

....

....

....

....

Date: .... Time: ....

Air Temp: ....

Location: ....

Launch Point: ....

Type:
Canal ☐ Sea ☐
River ☐ Lake ☐

Weather:
☀ ☐   ☁ ☐
⛅ ☐   🌧 ☐
☁ ☐   🌧 ☐

Details:

Statistics:
Distance:
Time:

Difficulty:
Beginner ——— Challenging
○ ○ ○ ○ ○

Conditions:
....
....
....
....
....

Date: .... Time: ....

Air Temp: ....

Location: ....

Launch Point: ....

Type: Canal ☐ Sea ☐ River ☐ Lake ☐

Weather: ☀ ☐ ☁ ☐ ⛅ ☐ 🌧 ☐ ☁ ☐ 🌧 ☐

Details:

Statistics:

Distance:

Time:

Difficulty:

Beginner ———— Challenging

○ ○ ○ ○ ○

Conditions:

Date: .... Time: ....

Air Temp: ....

Location: ....

Launch Point: ....

Type:
Canal ☐ Sea ☐
River ☐ Lake ☐

Weather:
☀ ☐   ☁ ☐
⛅ ☐   🌧 ☐
☁ ☐   🌧 ☐

Details:

Statistics:
Distance:
Time:

Conditions:
....
....
....
....
....

Difficulty:
Beginner ———— Challenging
○ ○ ○ ○ ○

Date: .... Time: ....

Air Temp: ....

Location: ....

Launch Point: ....

Type:
Canal ☐ Sea ☐
River ☐ Lake ☐

Weather:
☀ ☐ ☁ ☐
⛅ ☐ 🌧 ☐
☁ ☐ 🌧 ☐

Details:

Statistics:
Distance:
Time:

Difficulty:
Beginner ———— Challenging
○ ○ ○ ○ ○

Conditions:
....
....
....
....
....

Date: .... Time: ....

Air Temp: ....

Location: ....

Launch Point: ....

Type: Canal ☐ Sea ☐ River ☐ Lake ☐

Weather: ☀ ☐ ☁ ☐ ⛅ ☐ 🌧 ☐ ☁ ☐ 🌧 ☐

Details:

Statistics:

Distance:

Time:

Conditions:

Difficulty:

Beginner ——————— Challenging

◯ ◯ ◯ ◯ ◯

Date: .... Time: ....

Air Temp: ....

Location: ....

Launch Point: ....

Type:

Canal ☐ Sea ☐
River ☐ Lake ☐

Weather:

☀ ☐   ☁ ☐
⛅ ☐   🌧 ☐
☁ ☐   🌧 ☐

Details:

Statistics:

Distance:

Time:

Difficulty:

Beginner ———— Challenging

○ ○ ○ ○ ○

Conditions:

....

....

....

....

....

Date: .... Time: ....

Air Temp: ....

Location: ....

Launch Point: ....

Canal ☐   Sea ☐
River ☐   Lake ☐

Weather:

☀ ☐   ☁ ☐
⛅ ☐   🌧 ☐
☁ ☐   🌧 ☐

Details:

Statistics:

Distance:

Time:

Conditions:

....

....

....

....

....

Difficulty:

Beginner ———— Challenging

◯ ◯ ◯ ◯ ◯

Date: .... Time: ....

Air Temp: ....

Location: ....

Launch Point: ....

Type:
Canal ☐ Sea ☐
River ☐ Lake ☐

Weather:
☀ ☐   ☁ ☐
⛅ ☐   🌧 ☐
☁ ☐   🌨 ☐

Details:

Statistics:

Distance:

Time:

Conditions:

....

....

....

....

....

Difficulty:

Beginner ——————— Challenging

◯ ◯ ◯ ◯ ◯

Date: .... Time: ....

Canal ☐ Sea ☐
River ☐ Lake ☐

Air Temp: ....

Weather:
☀ ☐   ☁ ☐
⛅ ☐   🌧 ☐
☁ ☐   🌧 ☐

Location: ....

Launch Point: ....

Details:

Statistics:
Distance:
Time:

Conditions:
....
....

Difficulty:
Beginner ——————— Challenging
◯ ◯ ◯ ◯ ◯

....
....
....

Date: .... Time: ....

Air Temp: ....

Location: ....

Launch Point: ....

Type:

Canal ☐   Sea ☐
River ☐   Lake ☐

Weather:

☀ ☐   ☁ ☐
⛅ ☐   🌧 ☐
☁ ☐   🌧 ☐

Details:

Statistics:

Distance:

Time:

Difficulty:

Beginner ———— Challenging

○ ○ ○ ○ ○

Conditions:

....

....

....

....

....

Date: .... Time: ....

Air Temp: ....

Location: ....

Launch Point: ....

Type:
Canal ☐ Sea ☐
River ☐ Lake ☐

Weather:
☀ ☐   ☁ ☐
⛅ ☐   🌧 ☐
☁ ☐   🌧 ☐

Details:

Statistics:

Distance:

Time:

Difficulty:

Beginner ——————— Challenging

◯ ◯ ◯ ◯ ◯

Conditions:

....

....

....

....

....

Date: .... Time: ....

Air Temp: ....

Location: ....

Launch Point: ....

Type:

Canal ☐	Sea ☐
River ☐	Lake ☐

Weather:

☀ ☐   ☁ ☐
⛅ ☐   🌧 ☐
☁ ☐   🌧 ☐

Details:

Statistics:

Distance:

Time:

Conditions:

....

....

....

....

....

Difficulty:

Beginner ————— Challenging

○ ○ ○ ○ ○

Date: _____ Time: _____

Type:
Canal ☐ Sea ☐
River ☐ Lake ☐

Air Temp: _____

Weather:
☀ ☐   ☁ ☐
⛅ ☐   🌧 ☐
☁ ☐   🌧 ☐

Location: _____

Launch Point: _____

Details:

Statistics:

Distance:

Time:

Difficulty:

Beginner ——————— Challenging

◯ ◯ ◯ ◯ ◯

Conditions:

_____

_____

_____

_____

_____

Date: .... Time: ....

Air Temp: ....

Location: ....

Launch Point: ....

Type:

Canal	☐	Sea	☐
River	☐	Lake	☐

Weather:

☀	☐	☁	☐
⛅	☐	🌧	☐
☁	☐	🌧	☐

Details:

Statistics:

Distance:

Time:

Difficulty:

Beginner ———— Challenging

○ ○ ○ ○ ○

Conditions:

....

....

....

....

....

Date: _____ Time: _____

Air Temp: _____

Location: _____

Launch Point: _____

Type:
Canal ☐ Sea ☐
River ☐ Lake ☐

Weather:
☀ ☐   ☁ ☐
⛅ ☐   🌧 ☐
☁ ☐   🌧 ☐

Details:

Statistics:

Distance:

Time:

Conditions:

_____

_____

_____

Difficulty:

Beginner ——————— Challenging

◯ ◯ ◯ ◯ ◯

_____

_____

Date: .... Time: ....

Air Temp: ....

Location: ....

Launch Point: ....

Type:
Type:

Canal ☐ Sea ☐
River ☐ Lake ☐

Weather:

☀ ☐   ☁ ☐
⛅ ☐   🌧 ☐
☁ ☐   🌧 ☐

Details:

Statistics:

Distance:

Time:

Conditions:

....

....

....

....

....

Difficulty:

Beginner ———— Challenging

◯ ◯ ◯ ◯ ◯

Date: .... Time: ....

Canal ☐   Sea ☐
River ☐   Lake ☐

Air Temp: ....

Location: ....

Launch Point: ....

Weather:

☀ ☐   ☁ ☐
⛅ ☐   🌧 ☐
☁ ☐   🌧 ☐

Details:

Statistics:

Distance:

Time:

Conditions:

....

....

....

....

....

Difficulty:

Beginner ——————— Challenging

◯ ◯ ◯ ◯ ◯

Date: .... Time: ....

Air Temp: ....

Location: ....

Launch Point: ....

Type:
Canal ☐ Sea ☐
River ☐ Lake ☐

Weather:
☀ ☐   ☁ ☐
⛅ ☐   🌧 ☐
☁ ☐   🌧 ☐

Details:

Statistics:

Distance:

Time:

Difficulty:

Beginner ———— Challenging

○ ○ ○ ○ ○

Conditions:

....

....

....

....

....

Date: .... Time: ....

Air Temp: ....

Location: ....

Launch Point: ....

Type:

Canal ☐ Sea ☐
River ☐ Lake ☐

Weather:

☀ ☐   ☁ ☐
⛅ ☐   🌧 ☐
☁ ☐   🌧 ☐

Details:

Statistics:

Distance:

Time:

Difficulty:

Beginner ———— Challenging

○ ○ ○ ○ ○

Conditions:

....

....

....

....

....

Date: .... Time: ....

Air Temp: ....

Location: ....

Launch Point: ....

Type:
Canal ☐ Sea ☐
River ☐ Lake ☐

Weather:
☀ ☐   ☁ ☐
⛅ ☐   🌧 ☐
☁ ☐   🌧 ☐

Details:

Statistics:

Distance:

Time:

Difficulty:

Beginner ———— Challenging

○ ○ ○ ○ ○

Conditions:

....

....

....

....

....

Printed in Great Britain
by Amazon